Capitalism: what's the point?

A pioneering book about
sustainable economics,
sustainable business
and sustainable finance

Joss Tantram

TOWARDS 9 **BILLION**

A series of thoughts, provocations and
big ideas for a sustainable future

Book 1

© Copyright Joss Tantram/Terrafiniti LLP

ISBN: 978-0-9935952-0-2

Second edition 2017.

All rights reserved. No part of this book may be reproduced in any form or by any electronic or mechanical means including information storage and retrieval systems – except in the case of brief quotations in articles or reviews – without the permission in writing from its publisher.

This book is part of a series supporting Terrafiniti's thought leadership and information initiative, Towards 9 Billion.

About the author

Joss Tantram FRSA, FICRS is an expert in sustainable strategy and innovation, with more than 20 years' experience in the private and not-for-profit sectors in the UK, Europe and worldwide. Joss frequently contributes to leading sustainability websites including: Guardian Sustainable Business, 2degrees, Green Futures, Sustainable Brands, Toronto Sustainability Speaker Series, HuffPost Green, Blue & Green Tomorrow and Green Conduct. He blogs at: www.terrafiniti.com/blog

In praise of the author and Terrafiniti's Towards 9 Billion initiative

"Towards 9 Billion addresses the critical issues that face our planet in the 21st century, from business and economics to sustainable energy and technology. I love its wide-ranging intelligence, lucid prose and interdisciplinary approach to scoping a new economics for our age."
Jane Gleeson-White, author of 'Six Capitals, or Can Accountants Save the Planet: Rethinking Capitalism for the Twenty-First Century'

"Terrafiniti continues to not only pose the most important questions of our time - namely, how do we sustain and thrive on a planet of 9 billion people - but also proposes some fantastic ideas as to how we might do just that. A must read for anybody interested in where the planet is headed, and finding solutions to our most pressing challenges."
Jeremy Leggett, author, environmentalist, activist and solar pioneer

"Terrafiniti's Towards 9 Billion book series asks the important questions that lie beneath the accelerating chaos of systems no longer fit for purpose. We ignore them at our peril. They provide insightful analysis and innovative solutions which help us see the reality of the challenge, and the hope for change, through a clear lens. I hope these important contributions are widely read."
John Fullerton, Founder and President, Capital Institute

"The doughnut of social and planetary boundaries highlights the scale of the challenge humanity faces. Terrafiniti's Towards 9 Billion is a fount of refreshing ideas for surmounting that challenge, imagining economics, finance and enterprise for a flourishing future."
Kate Raworth, creator of Doughnut Economics and Senior Visiting Research Associate, Environmental Change Institute, Oxford University

"Big ideas for massive challenges: Terrafiniti's Towards 9 Billion provides a wide range of solution-oriented perspectives on the prospect – often seen as daunting – of accommodating 9 billion people within the remits of our one planet."
David Nussbaum, Chief Executive, WWF-UK

"Substance, originality and wisdom are the qualities that characterise Terrafiniti's Towards 9 Billion work. To all those who are disenchanted and even terrified by the lack of a coherent global approach to achieving sustainable development, take heart from Towards 9 Billion. Joss and Dominic have the courage and intellectual depth to face and articulate the most relevant and sometimes uncomfortable questions of our time."
Lois Guthrie, Founding Director, Carbon Disclosure Standards Board

"Suspect the future's going to be very different? Unsure how multiple economic, social and environmental forces will collide? But too little time to explore? Well treat yourself to a Towards 9 billion e-book. Short, sharp, accessible insights on what the future might look like and how you should prepare for it."
Mike Barry, Director, Plan A, Marks & Spencer

"I especially like Terrafiniti's thinking about sustainability, finance and economics: the idea of compounding instead of discounting, and the approach to Earth as a 'going concern', are deeply thought-provoking. So is their broader concept of a sustainable economy as a 'rejuvenative' enterprise. Terrafiniti's Towards 9 Billion blog articles have been an excellent resource for my students and for me as a teacher and advocate of sustainable development."
Ian Christie, Fellow of the Centre for Environmental Strategy at the University of Surrey and Associate of Green Alliance

"This series of well written and fun-illustrated books enables us to see the real possibilities for progressive change in capitalism, energy production, technology and enterprise as well as moral philosophy. It is a visionary package which contains the basis for escape from our present dilemmas. It needs to be read and acted upon."
Tim O'Riordan, Emeritus Professor of Environmental Sciences, University of East Anglia

"Building a sustainable future will take evolution and revolution, mixing what already works and challenging what does not. Terrafiniti's Towards 9 Billion creates positive, playful ideas which help us describe and drive a future where we and our planet can flourish together."
KoAnn Vikoren Skrzyniarz, Founder and Chief Executive, Sustainable Brands

"9 billion people living within ecological limits requires us to rethink and redesign our human systems so that they are in tune with natural systems. To do this we need both critical thinking and generative solutions that are rooted in purpose, inclusivity and creativity. Towards 9 Billion e-book series is an important contribution to humanity's great transition to a thriving planet earth."
Jen Morgan, Co-Founder, The Finance Innovation Lab

"Terrafiniti's Towards 9 Billion initiative raises powerful questions, and some equally powerful answers. Their sharp thinking combines a rational approach to analyse, in a subtle way, the wicked problems of our complex and rapidly changing world for the common good of present and future generations. Read this book, and read it again when you have finished it."
Alain Ruche, Senior Advisor to the Secretary-General of the EU External Service

"Terrafiniti's Towards 9 Billion is a creative approach for putting people and the planet at the heart of value. By pushing the boundaries of our thinking it poses serious questions and argues that the seeds of the future may already lie within our current, unsustainable approaches."
Jeremy Nicholls, Chief Executive, Social Value UK

"Few commentators on sustainability understand just how important compound interest and its reciprocal in the discount rate are in driving an unsustainable future. By normalising discounting as a means of investment appraisal we discount the children's future. We turn the world into a cog within the financial machine. Joss Tantram's book draws attention to this matter, meriting close attention."
Alastair McIntosh, author of 'Soil and Soul'

"Terrafiniti's Towards 9 Billion is a source of innovation and inspiration for a future fit for the planet and people. Its mix of thinking about how the world could be and exploration of the tools and techniques we have at our disposal right now is an invaluable aid to all of us working for a sustainable world."
David Pencheon, Head of NHS Sustainable Development Unit

"A fascinating approach to a challenging subject."
Cary Krosinsky, noted author, educator and advisor on business, sustainability and investing

"It's crazy to imagine a world of 9 billion people. Right now it's even crazier to ignore how we're going to deal with each other on such a crowded planet. Uncomfortably, we have to adopt Terrafiniti's thinking."
Professor Michael Mainelli, Chairman, Z/Yen Group

Introduction

This book is all about questions, but also about answers. Some are big and some are small. Some are about the nature and purpose of our systems of value, and some about how we value our loved ones. Sometimes the smallest questions have the biggest answers.

Human beings are great at asking questions. We start off very good indeed. Children's ability to identify questions and their commitment to asking them often outstrips our ability to answer them. It is not merely that an incessant stream of 'why' questions is tiring it's also that some of the time we genuinely don't know the answers to the questions we are asked or are unprepared to deal with their true implications.

As we grow up we often keep questioning, but the scope of those questions can narrow due to the practical need to balance a sense of wonder with passing an exam or earning an income. We still question aspects of life but often the questions are more about the details and less about the overall purpose. This 'bounded rationality' keeps our questions within a less examined frame of reference and is one of the challenges our species faces in breaking away from unsustainable ways of being and creating new ones that may differ slightly or radically.

Why so many questions?
In simple terms, sustainability is about one of two things: *doing the same things very differently* or doing *very different things*.

Maintaining our status quo commits us to a collision course with the very real limits to possibility on this wonderful though populous planet. To follow a path to sustainability we need to ask and then answer some fundamental questions of economics, finance and business. Not just 'can we do business with less impact?' - but 'how do we connect finance with a flourishing future in the first place?'

Over previous centuries immense logic and ingenuity have been applied in the creation of our systems of value and enterprise. However, we face challenges which require a rejuvenation of our thinking because the logic of the past often falls short of the obstacles of the future.

Unless we ask the big questions - 'what is the point of capitalism?' and 'how do we value a sustainable future?' - we will

Contents
09 What's the point of capitalism?
12 Planetisation of finance: the Earth as a going concern

COUNTERPOINT
19 How much is your Mother (Earth) worth?
22 Sensational! Against the tide of shallow value

BIG IDEAS
29 Discounting the discount rate

BIG IDEAS
34 Calm down - it's only lustrum trading
38 Glossary
39 UN SDGs cross reference table
40 Further reading

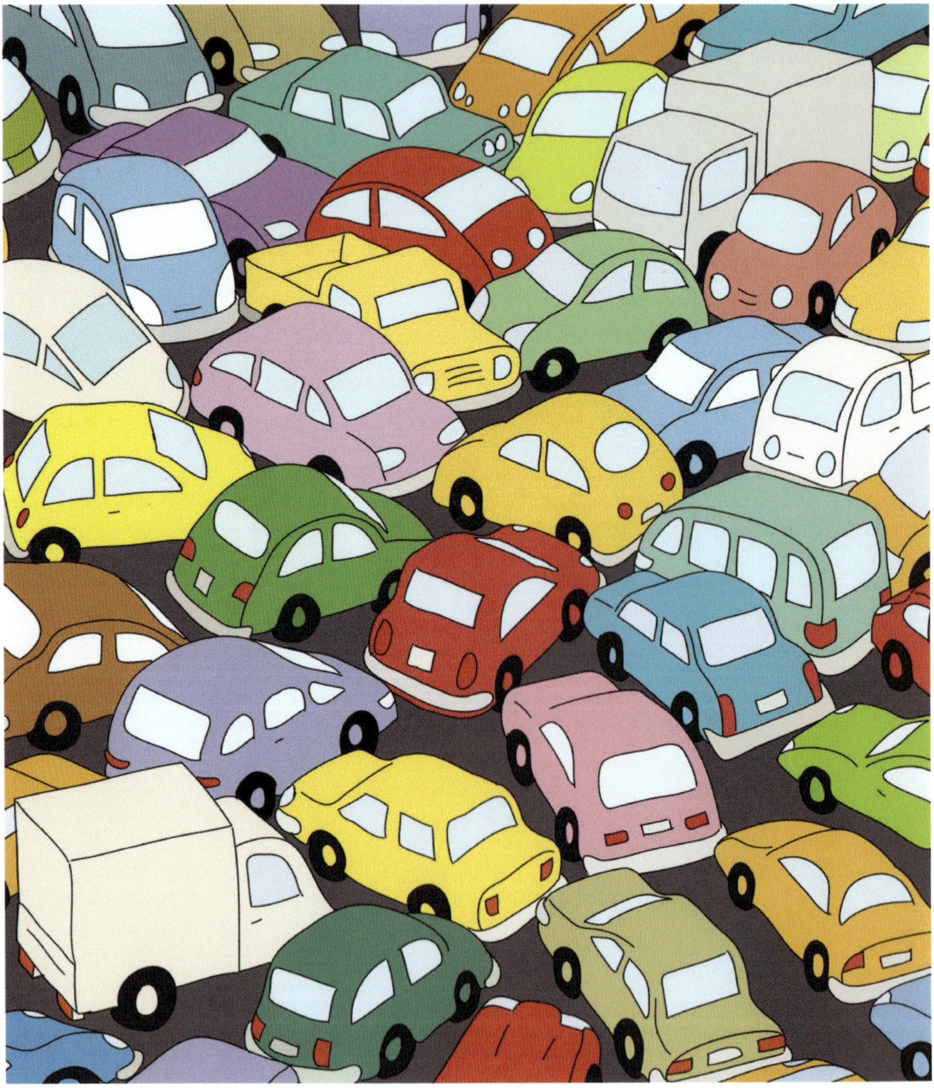

be unlikely to find answers which meet the scale of the challenge.

The current rules of the game for capitalism are undermining its own long-term existence. Any game includes winners and losers, creativity, luck, cooperation and competition, and should do so in order to deliver creativity, innovation and the chance of individual and collective choice, reward and wellbeing.

Changing the rules such that capitalism seeks to deliver sustainability wouldn't affect the range of possible outcomes and types of choices within the game. Indeed, it would help ensure that we all had more chance to play for longer, and indeed might guarantee that more of us might 'win'.

Systems of economics, capitalism and enterprise that sustain us are required and beloved, but also feared and doubted

Why is this book necessary?

This book is about some big questions about the nature of things and some naïve questions as to whether things must be as they are.

Humans tend to love and despise systems in equal measure. The systems of economics, capitalism and enterprise that sustain us are required and beloved, but also feared and doubted.

This book is intended to provide readers with new ideas and hopefully some inspiration about how we might think differently about a sustainable future and the route to achieving it.

It asks why our systems of value and production function the way they do and whether they must always do the same. It questions just how our markets give rise to behaviour so perverse that it's in no one's interest to leave them untouched. It explores the idea that there might be a purpose behind these systems and that we might aspire to more human approaches for the good of our home and our species.

This book is an exploration of what might be possible if we are brave enough to ask the big questions: 'do our current systems of value contain the seeds of the next ones?' 'must profit for one always mean loss for another?' 'how do we move to a positive sum economy, where common good and private interest naturally align?'.

Our goal in producing this book, and the others in the series, is to put ideas out into the world. Just as plants and animals broadcast seed and progeny in vast numbers in the hope that some will survive and flourish, we hope that our ideas might have the chance to find receptive places in which to thrive.

What's next?

This book, drawn from the writing on our Towards 9 Billion blog, is one of a series that we hope will grow over time, producing big, hopeful ideas for an equitable, sustainable world.

At its heart, Towards 9 Billion asks the following question: what if we could welcome 9 billion people rather than fear their arrival? If you want to read more, have a look at our blog www.terrafiniti.com/blog.

If you like what you read here and want to talk, discuss, explore or find out more, please get in touch with us.

What's the point of capitalism?

> "Every step and every movement of the multitude, even in what are termed enlightened ages, are made with equal blindness to the future; and nations stumble upon establishments, which are indeed the result of human action, but not the execution of any human design."
>
> Adam Ferguson

Capitalism has no stated end goal, no clear intention or purpose, yet it dominates our planet; increasingly defining the prevailing norms of public policy enterprise, social life and even ethics. This lack of purpose should be of great concern. Yet bizarrely, more and more effort is poured into preserving our erratic stumbling from one crisis to another. Just as the strategic challenges[1] of a populous, increasingly consuming and polluted planet become ever more clear, so the capitalist response seems to be 'leave me alone, I'm busy just now'.

We really ought to require a little more from our operating system - capitalism needs a purpose

A tactical planet
Who would run an enterprise on tactics but no strategy? Of course, governments have, over the last two decades, substituted reaction to headlines for any long-term vision, but companies are thought to have a more strategic perspective. Global business leaders are lauded as 'visionary', 'far-sighted' and 'prophetic'. All such terms are associated with the idea of moving beyond short-term reaction to events, indicating an ability to read the runes, see the way the world is going and to envision and enact activities strategically over the long term.

If this is a quality that we value, or at least aspire to value, why is it not a characteristic we also seek in the world's defacto operating system? If capitalism has no strategic intent, why are we so comfortable letting it drive our future?

Just what is the point of capitalism?

No direction, just travel
Capitalism is like a spaceship with no long-range maps, not seeking an ultimate destination, valuing only the journey itself.

Of course philosophically we can tell ourselves that the journey is the destination, but given the clear picture that is emerging[2] of the place that business-as-usual capitalism is taking us, it is becoming increasingly difficult just to relax and enjoy the ride.

Why are we in thrall to a system which recognises no common outcomes and which intends nothing except the agglomeration of an abstracted indicator (capital) regardless of its provenance or the sustainability and longevity of its foundations?

Capitalism works (for some)
There is significant focus at present on a post-millennial recapitulation of Marx's analysis of international capitalism. For instance, Thomas Piketty's *Capital in the Twenty-First Century*[3], asks (and answers) whether capitalism works[4], and if so, for whom.

If you were to ask the world's 85 richest people on a bus (as described by Oxfam)[5], they might well say 'well, it works for me'. Indeed you could probably count on around another one and a half billion saying 'it works for us and we hope it might work harder in future'.

The rest of humanity might still have a faint hope that capitalism is their best bet for personal enrichment and security.

Capitalism does work. However, it works much, much better for some than others, and it works best for a very small number of us and not at all for many of the planet's other species.

Like a rolling stone

For the bus passengers above, capitalism is a bit like rolling a stone downhill; you do best if you live at the top and have access to stones.

Live at the bottom of the hill though and the stones will either be mostly static or coming downhill on a collision course with your house or your foot.

If so, your opportunities to benefit from the natural ease with which stones roll downhill will be severely compromised. Some living at the bottom of the hill will of course, through luck and/or hard work, make their way to the top. Generally though, where you start plays a defining role in where you end up.[6]

What *is* the point?

We really ought to require a little more from our operating system - capitalism needs a purpose. It doesn't have to be much, just some intended outcome that we might judge and assess behaviour against, perhaps something simple such as...'a sustainable and equitable world for humanity.'

We shouldn't demand anything too prescriptive that would get in the way of creativity or entrepreneurial spirit, just something to indicate a clear direction and possible destination for the good of us all.

Within this context some people would of course do better than others – this is capitalism we are talking about, not communism. It's just that a planetary operating system should be useful to the people who are part of it, not just those lucky enough to live right at the top of the rocky hill.

What's the point of capitalism? It's time we made up our minds.

Further reading (also see p.40)
1. The Millennium Project: Global Futures Studies & Research
2. Global Risks 2014 Insight Report, World Economic Forum
3. Capital in the Twenty-First Century, Thomas Piketty
4. Capitalism simply isn't working and here are the reasons why, Will Hutton, The Guardian
5. Working for the Few: Political capture and economic inequality, Oxfam
6. Sutton Trust report on Educational Background of Professions in the UK

Planetisation of finance: the Earth as a going concern

> *"We have statesmen and politicians who profess to guide our destinies. Whither are they guiding our destinies?"*
> H.G. Wells

In recent decades considerable effort has been invested in describing and identifying the planet's natural environment in terms that can be understood and integrated into the language of economics and finance – from the 1997 work of Robert Constanza et al[1], the TEEB[2] coalition and the Natural Capital Coalition[3], to the multi-capitals approaches to accounting and reporting that are forming part of efforts by organisations such as the Sustainability Accounting Standards Board[4] and the International Integrated Reporting Council[5]. Each is seeking to quantify and therefore consider the value of natural systems and their outputs in comparable financial terms.

I have written extensively on these approaches, mostly from the perspective of a critical friend rather than wide-eyed fan, and mostly because I feel that the conceptualisation of natural and social capital into economic terms will lead to a commodification of nature (a financialisation of the planet) unless there is radical change to the nature and purpose of global markets (the planetisation of finance).

In order to move beyond a critical analysis of the pros and cons of the multi-capitals approach, it seems to me that there is a simpler, pre-existing conceptual vehicle that could be adopted to provide a forward-looking perspective on the value of the planet and its assets (natural, human, built and otherwise).

This is the concept of the going concern, an accounting approach to assessing the value of an enterprise based upon its potential for continuing existence. It is at the heart of our thought experiment to explore an IPO (Initial Public Offering) for the Earth[6], a finalist in the ICAEW/Accounting for Sustainability Finance for the Future Awards 2014.

Planetisation of finance: the Earth as a going concern 13

Opportunity costs (and benefits)
Approaches to the valuation of currently under-represented or under-priced sources of capital (those which are not pure financial capital) predominantly focus upon two aspects of value: capital stocks and capital flows. A simple metaphor for these two categories is that of a bank account, where the stock is the money in the account and the flow is the interest that is generated by the capital.

I would argue that there is a more significant area worthy of attention: the going concern value that the existence of healthy stocks and flows gives rise to. This is not the value of the stock or flow itself, but is derived from the opportunities that become possible because of the existence of the stocks and flows.

When viewed through this lens, natural capital becomes most powerful not when it is used to give rise to an asset value calculation (what would we get if we sell it?), but a going concern value (what does the asset's continued existence and health allow us to do and how valuable is that?).

This distinction between asset price and the value of the opportunities that arise from the asset is partially reflected in the concept of stocks and flows. But the idea of a going concern value goes beyond a flow valuation. An example of these category differences for a company like Google would be as follows:
- Asset value – the market capitalisation of the company (what it would fetch if it were sold)
- Asset flow value – the yearly revenue of the company
- Going concern value – in addition to the categories above, the value of all the things that exist because Google provides and facilitates fertile ground for a huge range of activity.

Valuing our planet as a going concern
If the motivation behind approaches to valuing natural, social and other capitals is to highlight their value to the economy rather than consider them as economic externalities, shouldn't we take a more creative approach to using the accounting techniques that already exist? Wouldn't it be far more productive to consider the value of the planet as a going concern – as a place to do sustainable business over the long term?

Luckily, there is a well-established approach to doing just that. Accountants do it all the time. All we need to do is expand its scope and scale somewhat, from the going concern value of a specific entity to the going (common) concern value of the planet as a whole. In accountancy, the going concern principle is the assumption that an entity will remain in business for the foreseeable future. If it can be assumed that a business will remain viable over time, it can be considered to be valuable because of its capacity to sustain economic activity. 'The value of an entity that is assumed to be a going concern is higher than its breakup value, since a going concern can potentially continue to earn profits'[7].

> **The task in front of us is to move from the financialisation of the planet to the planetisation of finance**

Going for how long?
While it may seem perverse to say so, in cold mechanistic terms the Earth's value to humans lies in providing us with the means to carry on doing stuff – not in either its inherent value (what we would pay to keep it) or its value when broken up and traded (what we would get if we sold it). The idea of planetary going concern value is too often ignored, partly because it asks us to project value into the future. In accounting terms, going concern assessments focus upon a consideration of 'the foreseeable future', but this is only judged using a one year forward time horizon (aligned to annual accounting and reporting).

At a planetary scale, an annual going concern perspective wouldn't get us very far. We need to be thinking about how to project the value of a going concern much further, say to 2050.

Such projections happen for smaller things all the time. The world is full of news stories and analysis saying 'the market for X could be worth $10 billion by 2025' or 'sales of Y set to grow by 200% over the next ten years'. All such projections assume a continuation of certain elements of business as usual (i.e. a similarly functioning market to today's) and certain elements of change (e.g. increased disposable income, increased urbanisation, etc.) that are interpreted from various trend analyses and forecasts.

> Without a reconsideration of what constitutes sustainable value, we are just building ever more rickety structures

At the planetary scale, a going concern calculation could be done for a range of scenarios, e.g. where no significant strategic response is made so as to evolve to meet the challenges of pressurised resources, consumption increase, reduction in soil fertility, increased pollution and climate uncertainty, as opposed to the planetary enterprise that would be possible if we made the transition to a sustainable economy fit for 9 billion interdependent citizens, all capable of making sovereign social and economic decisions.

It seems clear that the former would, by its nature, be less valuable than the latter.

Not under current management

Accountants judge a going concern according to a range of criteria that could easily be adapted to apply to the planet as a whole. The Financial Reporting Council's Statement of Auditing Standards[8] on the issue in 1994 states that, for financial audits seeking to judge whether an entity is a going concern, the following should be taken into consideration:

- Whether the period to which the directors have paid particular attention in assessing going concern is reasonable in the entity's circumstances and in the light of the need for the directors to consider the ability of the entity to continue in operational existence for the foreseeable future;
- The systems, or other means (formal or informal), for timely identification of warnings of future risks and uncertainties the entity might face;
- Budget and/or forecast information (cash flow information in particular) produced by the entity;
- Whether the key assumptions underlying the budgets and/or forecasts appear appropriate in the circumstances;
- The sensitivity of budgets and/or forecasts to variable factors both within the control of the directors and outside their control;
- The existence, adequacy and terms of borrowing facilities, and supplier credit; and

- The directors' plans for resolving any matters giving rise to the concern (if any) about the appropriateness of the going concern basis. In particular, the auditors may need to consider whether the plans are realistic, whether there is a reasonable expectation that the plans are likely to resolve any problems foreseen and whether the directors are likely to put the plans into practice effectively.

If a planetary-scale auditor used the criteria above to assess the current defacto administration of the planet (our economic and market systems), would they judge the Earth to be a going concern, and if so, for how long? Is the simple but frightening answer that the Earth is not capable of being considered to be a going concern over the coming decades under current management?

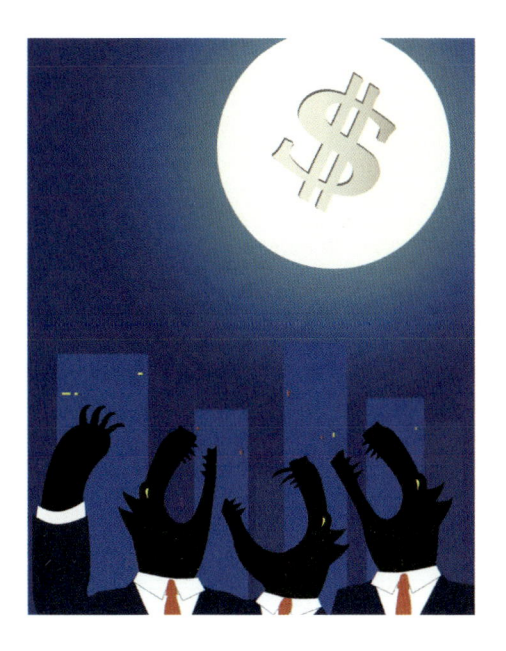

Towards a planetisation of finance

> *"The twelfth law is that such things as cannot be divided, be enjoyed in common…"*
> Thomas Hobbes' 12th Law

The vast majority of approaches to bring under-priced or unpriced capitals within financial domains tend to do so by treating them as adjustments to existing prices (e.g. as carbon taxes) rather than focusing upon and questioning the origination of their price in the first place.

Externalities should not be priced per se. However, price must reflect them (they shouldn't really be externalities at all, just a fundamental aspect of costs that should be naturally recognised) if any approach to building a sustainable economy is to succeed.

The point of exploring the planetary going concern concept is to provide another driver towards the more innate consideration of sustainability as a defining aspect of financial success over the long term. The planet can only be considered a going concern if such fundamental dependencies are integrated into the heart of decision-making, not considered after the fact as most current approaches to 'pricing externalities' currently require. Without a fundamental reconsideration of what actually constitutes sustainable value, and an effort to align the origination of money (and price) against that, we are just building ever more rickety structures upon the already unsteady foundations of current economic and market processes.

Valuing the planet in economic terms runs the risk of financialising, commodifying and privatising nature. The task in front of us is not to tinker with the methods, but to reverse this concept, moving from the financialisation of the planet to the planetisation of finance.

Economics and markets based upon the value of the planet as a going concern might be a powerful and positive step towards aligning financial value with the physical facts of life on this planet – the only place we have (as yet) do to business.

Further reading (also see p.40)
1. The Value of the World's Ecosystem Services and Natural Capital, Robert Costanza, Nature
2. TEEB: The Economics of Ecosystems and Biodiversity
3. The Natural Capital Coalition
4. Conceptual Framework of the Sustainability Accounting Standards Board
5. Capitals Background Paper for <IR>, International Integrated Reporting Council
6. Earth Public Offering project, Terrafiniti
7. The Going Concern Basis in Financial Reports, Financial Reporting Council
8. The Going Concern Principle, Accounting Tools
9. Six Capitals: The revolution capitalism has to have – or can accountants save the planet?, Jane Gleeson-White

My profuse thanks go to Jane Gleeson-White[9] for her feedback and comments on a draft of this article. Any errors of logic or hyperbole are unquestionably mine.

COUNTERPOINT

4/7

How much is your Mother (Earth) worth?

"All human things of dearest value hang on slender strings."
Edmund Waller

So you want to sell your mother. It's a free market; most other things are bought and sold these days and all sorts of exotic items are priced and traded every second.

You reckon she must be worth a decent amount. I mean, she is your mum after all! How to figure out the asking price though? That's where it starts to get tricky.

Assuming you like her, you may feel that she is worth more than a simple calculation of what you might fetch with the sale of her possessions, the change and notes in her purse and the sum of selling off any decent stuff she owns.

Similarly, selling her house, car and savings or investments (if she has them) may well not come close to telling you how much she ought to fetch. It is possible that you may be able to calculate what her actions are worth. For example, start with your existence value (you're obviously worth a lot and she brought you into the world after all) then tot up all the services she provided you over the years (physical and emotional support, etc.) and then add all the stuff she's bought you, such as food and clothes. She's probably done a whole load of stuff for other people too, so add something in to cover that as well.

The trouble is that if you take this approach you may be left with a nagging feeling that you have sold yourself (and perhaps your dear old mum) rather short.

The Earth presents a pretty similar challenge for pricing. You can price its results and its productivity, but that price comes nowhere near a true reflection of the value of its capacity to continue to sustain us and everything else in (pretty much) perpetuity.

This is why the seductive notion of pricing ecosystems as a route to sustainability must be seen clearly for what it is and what it is not.

Using a comparable metric like money as a way to put things on a level playing field makes sense, but only up to a point. Such an approach would be fine if the things we were comparing were truly comparable. However, the environment is something you can't do without.

There is a dependency relationship. Put simply, there is no money without human beings capable of inventing and using it. There are no human beings without food, air and water.

If you can't measure, you can't be bothered
The logic of ecosystem valuation is motivated by the idea that we need to value and price the contribution our economy gets from the natural world; once that value is identified, it can be considered and balanced alongside other priorities.

Value implies price, price implies sales, and sales imply markets.

If we are not careful we will reduce everything to money and lose sight of the real value we started with.

The idea that: if we can't measure it we can't manage it pervades much of our current way of prioritising activity. However, there are many cases when it simply does not either apply or help. For instance, how do you quantify the love you feel for your children, your parents or partner? You don't. You know the value without needing to know the quantity. Finding an exact figure is irrelevant, pointless and borderline offensive.

In essence the trouble with pricing the priceless is that it implies fungibility (economic 'swapability'). By putting a price on your mother, you are essentially saying that you'd be equally happy with a different one that cost the same.

Valuing the invaluable
Breaking down the value of your mother into monetary amounts based on the individual benefits she brings to your life will ultimately sorely undervalue her; such is the dilemma presented by the move towards valuing ecosystem services.

Factoring the Earth's ability to sustain us into economic value is a little more complex than just finding a price that we would be prepared to pay or forgo to preserve or develop parts of the environment.

Ecosystem prices tell us what it would be worth if we sold all of our mum's stuff - but it wouldn't buy us a new Mother (Earth).

We have produced a short animated video to illustrate this idea.
You can find it at www.terrafiniti.com/blog/valuing-natural-capital-and-selling-your-mother-the-remix

5/7
Sensational! Against the tide of shallow value

> "What does the world weigh? Its scales are crooked. It weighs life
> and labor in the balance against silver and gold. That will never
> balance, it spills a lot of life that way."
> Walter M. Miller Jnr, *A Canticle for Liebowitz*

Real value refers to those things which have meaning in sustaining and supporting life, whether human or otherwise.

Shallow value refers to value priced beyond its worth, where value is the product of hype, glitter and market hysteria rather than of human and ecological need or meaning.

It is time to value what is precious to us all: the water, food and air that give us life, the shelter and warmth that allow comfort, the security of place, equitable income, education and communication that allow us to plan for our and our children's future and the ability to develop, share, discuss and distribute ideas about the world and our existence.

Swamped by shallow value

Shallow value dominates our media, our discourse and our markets. It is the triumph of sensation over meaning, surface over depth and gratification over satisfaction. It is by no means restricted to the obvious and literal elevation of image over substance in the media but has increasingly pervaded the everyday, becoming the base currency of capitalism itself and influencing the very core of how we understand and value what is worthwhile.

Capitalism has come to depend upon sensation to sell its products; brand has become the medium for translating a set of corporate behaviours, undertaken to maximise private profit, into a set of implied emotions and sensations. Buying a product or wearing a brand, capitalism implies, will help us to be who we want to be – to be happier, more beautiful, better and more fulfilled people.

Of course this is nothing new; sensational bubbles[1] have been a feature of markets for many hundreds of years. More explicitly, the foundations of modern advertising consciously used and adapted the then emergent science of psychology for the purposes of linking products to a buyer's sense of self and self-worth.

Alastair McIntosh, the scholar and activist, has written extensively on the issue in relation to tobacco marketing and the pornography of consumerism. In his logical and emotional tour de force *Hell and High Water*[2], he summarises consumerism's deliberate "hacking" of psychological circuitry as follows: "Could this be the core dynamic by which consumerism sustains itself? Addictions are powerful precisely because they taunt us with our heart's longing. But they fake it. They short-circuit and actually block off the real thing – the focus of our ultimate concern."

Building upon McIntosh's thesis, I would argue that this sensationalist agenda has gone far further than merely representing the (now) unspoken design principles of advertising and marketing. It has also become unconsciously embedded within the very DNA of every facet of economic and financial activity, warping our conceptions of what is valuable, mistaking shallow economic price for real value.

The fetishisation of financial markets

One of the main reasons financial markets struggle with real value is the problem of economic externalities. These are the environmental, social and economic costs and benefits which either take place 'outside' institutional accounts or occur across the balance sheets of multiple actors, stakeholders or proxies. The reconciliation and adequate pricing of economic externalities has become a major source of activity for environmentalists and economists[3,4] seeking to address systemic and unpriced risks and market failures.

The problem of externalities becomes much, much more difficult when we consider the active disinterest of modern financial markets in their original, fundamental purpose. Financial markets first grew as a way of providing financial resources to agricultural and mercantile enterprise, allowing endeavours to be undertaken in expectation of future reward – for example, allowing a merchant to invest in stock for the next sea voyage in the expectation that the current one would land and its cargo be sold.

Financiers supporting such endeavours would of course need to make an assessment as to whether the investee in question was likely to be able to make good on the debt, and the way that they organised and conducted their business was therefore a key area of judgement for investors.

Today's listed company markets are theoretically no different, representing a set of companies seeking investment and requiring a judgement by investors as to whether those companies have the strategy, risk management and staff capabilities to execute that strategy and deliver a return on investment.

> It is time to value the abundance, vitality and interdependence of all that exists on this precious, irreplaceable planet

It may therefore be presumed that an interest in, and analysis of, the fundamental viability, utility and longevity of those companies would be an essential area of interest for investors. While this is certainly the case for a wide range of individual investors, it is not necessarily true for the market as a whole. Market movement and the behaviours and inferred intentions of other market actors have become more important than an analysis of company fundamentals.

Market movement has become king, because, with the rise of automatic, sub-second trading technologies, investors have become more interested in making sure they are not left stranded by market hysteria than acting as financiers and stewards of companies.

The UK economist John Kay entertainingly explores this fetishised market in his *Parable of the Ox*[5], which describes the perverse development of a market focused solely upon market actors (experts in the art of ox weighing) rather than upon its original purpose (weighing an actual ox).

I would additionally argue that beyond the pornography of marketing and advertising, beyond the mistaken belief that price equals value, beyond a focus upon the market rather than the investee, there is one further perversion of real value that we have allowed to take place: the belief that just because a thing *can* be traded, it should be.

The calculated sensationalism of price

"I conceive that the great part of the miseries of mankind are brought upon them by false estimates they have made of the value of things."

Benjamin Franklin

Price is not value itself; it is a signifier of value. However, it is one which largely omits the value of externalities. In sustainability terms, this is a problem because the major means of determining behaviour in our capitalist world is the price signal. We continue to knowingly explore and exploit dwindling and dangerous sources of non-renewable fuel because price perversely pushes us to, telling us that the use of free energy from the wind and the sun is somehow more expensive overall. Renewables are often currently more economically expensive, but the price of such fuels is not the same as their value to us.

Ceteris non paribus – all things are not equal

Efforts to define the price and value of natural capital can equally fall prey to confusion between price and value. We are easily lulled into the notion that if we price something we can make a rational decision to trade it and that it is somehow fungible – that the money we receive in return for a trade can be used to obtain a substitute which is functionally useful in the same way as the property traded in the first place.

Trading the stuff of life

Financial markets have become obsessed with shallow value and too remote for too long, from anything that resembles real life. Recent years have shown us just a fraction of the dangers of exotic financial instruments, of bundling up a range of debts, and labelling them as risk-free investments for trading long after we have forgotten the underlying value of the asset (or absence of asset) upon which they were originally based.

Shallow value is the triumph of sensation over meaning, surface over depth

Such abstraction goes far beyond the re-packaging of potentially bad debts. Financial markets have, in recent years, undertaken trading in food stuffs – the fundamental components of human survival[6] – for purposes far removed from the allocation and distribution of those assets to those in need of them.

This trade has become a sensational distortion of the purpose of markets in food stuffs, focused merely around the idea that the thing traded can give rise to profit, rather than that the thing traded can give rise to adequate nutrition.

Can life arise from poisoned markets?

"Capitalism is the astounding belief that the most wickedest of men will do the most wickedest of things for the greatest good of everyone."

John Maynard Keynes

In such a fetishised market, can the trading of environmental and natural value, through carbon credits, conservation banking credits, transferable development rights and other such theoretically sustainable finance instruments possibly give rise to the sort of long-term, strategic outcomes that our planet needs? Are they just another means by which common value can be turned into private profit?

Surely, if we are to truly use the mechanisms of capital markets and international trading to deliver environmental and social good then those markets need to be fundamentally reformed, such that they are capable of truly valuing a common future as more valuable than a private present.

Such markets must have both the incentive and capability to deliver the required strategic outcomes. They must rise to the challenge of valuing activities and behaviour which pay off over the long term, to compound rather than discount the value of a more sustainable future and to start to value decisions that allow the growth and stability of ecosystems and societies as an outcome of value to the market as a whole. Allowing sustainable decisions and behaviours to be inherently valued and prioritised rather than considered as an afterthought.

Truly sustainable markets – those dedicated to the discovery, trading and distribution of real value – would, therefore, naturally:
- Value abundance: consider the longevity and safety of supply of the resources they depend upon;
- Preserve and grow vitality: act to value and enhance the quality and diversity of the natural capital upon which human life depends; and
- Value and balance interdependence: prioritise mutual equity in relationships with suppliers, customers and other stakeholders.

It is time for real value. It is time to value the abundance, vitality and interdependence of all that exists on this precious, irreplaceable planet, to move beyond the surface, sensational value of current market price and start to define and trade the real value which sustains us all.

Further reading (also see p.40)
1. Market Bubbles, NYU Stern
2. Hell and High Water: Climate Change, Hope and the Human Condition, Alastair McIntosh
3. End This Depression Now!, Paul Krugman
4. The Price of Inequality: How Today's Divided Society Endangers Our Future, Joseph E. Stiglitz
5. The Parable of the Ox, John Kay
6. Food speculation, Global Justice Now

**BIG IDEAS
FOR A SUSTAINABLE FUTURE**

6/7

Discounting the discount rate

> *"We are made wise not by the recollection of our past, but by the responsibility for our future."*
> George Bernard Shaw

We know that a bird in the hand is worth two in the bush. The adage works well, and it makes sense for a hunter-gatherer. But does it also hold true for a globalised species seeking a sustainable future? Under some circumstances, might the bird in the hand actually be worth less than a larger number of birds which are potentially available but currently out of reach?

Does the value proposition change at four birds in the bush, at six, or at ten?

How do we value something we could have against what we have already?

Such questions abound as we focus upon one of the most fundamental challenges to the achievement of a sustainable and prosperous future: the lack of a functional economic mechanism to help us positively value the future.

Our financial measures predominantly focus upon the value of the immediate. There is of course a certain logic to valuing today more highly than we value next week or beyond – the present actually exists (for the sake of argument), while next week is only a logical probability. In any case, even if we could be sure that next week will exist, we have no idea what might happen between now and then, what new technologies would transform the opportunities we might have to catch birds, make bird substitutes, change our dependency upon birds, etc.

> Our conceptions of the meaning and purpose of money are no more fixed in stone or incapable of change than any other systems

Discounting our chances for a sustainable future

A consideration of future value is a key part of any investment decision, financial planning or accounting process. An amount of money in your hand can be considered definitely real (in as much as money is ever real), whereas money in the future is always considered to be less valuable as it is far more notional and conditional upon circumstances. This is referred to in terms of the discount that future value would have when set against its value now (net present value).

The mechanism for calculating this reduction of value over time is the discount rate. A seemingly innocent and rational accounting technique, the discount rate is perhaps the most significant reason why we find it so hard to invest in a sustainable future.

Some approaches exist which allow us to value future outcomes, yet each is substantially constrained by the deadening effect of the discount rate.

Cost benefit analysis, for instance, is the main vehicle for assessing the likely financial outcomes of different courses of action. It was used by Lord Stern[1] to calculate that the costs of a transition to a lower carbon economy were a fraction of those of dealing with the implications of unconstrained climate change.

Discounting future value makes a great deal of sense for many things but it also projects a restraint on forward planning that restricts adequate investment in sustainable change.

Like so many aspects of economics and accounting, it is intensely logical (and useful) within a very specific frame of reference. If that frame of reference shifts, then logic would dictate a reconsideration of its utility.

The frame of reference for the discount rate has definitively shifted.

From discounting to compounding

Economics, finance and accounting may not have developed mechanisms to compound value over time (as noted, because the future doesn't exist yet). However, it's conceivable to imagine a social and economic architecture that would innately involve an ability to compound the future.

There are a couple of possible ways to increase future value and therefore encourage behaviour which pays off over the long term. These are:

1. For there to be a purpose to capitalism
This solution is exquisitely easy to express, though perhaps rather harder to achieve. We need to introduce a long-term purpose for economic activity. In addition to being financially and personally worthwhile for individuals to participate in, economic activity

The discount rate dominates and dictates an unsustainable future because humanity does not have a plan

should make a manifest contribution to the achievement of both healthy and thriving ecosystems and a global human population of 9 billion capable citizens.

With these goals in place, it would be relatively easy to compound value and to judge behaviour by its contribution to these goals, asking the question 'are these activities likely to achieve or to undermine our sustainable destination?' Just as investors currently (in theory) assess the likelihood of a company achieving its stated aims and value it accordingly, so this could be done in the context of a shared long-term goal.

2. To change the rules of money (long money and short money)
This refers to ideas which either change the conception of money itself or which alter the rules that are applied to money.

One such approach to the rules of money would be to create 'slow/long money' and 'fast/short money'. Short money would have a use by date and be spent on day-to-day things. Long money would be more suited to infrastructure investment and projects with a long term or common-good payoff.

The mechanism for creating such distinctions exists; it is called demurrage. It is a reverse interest rate and refers to a cost levied for holding or owning money for a given period. Applying demurrage universally would naturally discourage people and organisations from sitting on money, and encourage its circulation or investment as long money which would be inherently more useful for the common good.

A practical example of this type of thinking is in the area of complementary currencies, which have been used in reality across the world in order to achieve a range of rather amazing things. A pioneer of alternative currencies is Bernard Lietaer[2]. His books and websites give a number of incredibly inspiring and creative examples as to how reconceptualising money can change the world and in many cases already has done.

We meant to save our civilisation but didn't have a budget code for the work
The discount rate dominates and dictates an unsustainable future because, surprisingly or not, humanity doesn't have a plan. As a species, we are old enough, and dangerous enough, not to be blundering around without a destination and a plan by which to get there.

A common direction is not dictatorship, communism or even collectivism. It is simply an intention to survive, and perhaps even to thrive, over the coming decades. Our current mode of capitalism is no less collectivist than what I propose; it defines shared modes of behaviour, measurement, legality and value. However, current capitalism lacks a definable and constructive plan for the prosperity of our species or planet over the long term. This is an issue which is manifestly worth addressing as it is clear that the demand is there; most of humanity[3] is keen to ensure a viable and successful future for themselves and their loved ones.

Likewise, our conceptions of the meaning and purpose of money are no more fixed in stone or incapable of change than any other systems (though they may have more inertia). Money is a tool, a means by which we signify value and facilitate exchange. Valuing the long-term success of our species should certainly be worth something and perhaps it is time we considered the role that our means of exchange could have in achieving that success.

The forthcoming challenges of sustainability should spur our action, so that we might design ways to overcome the barrier of the discount rate and work towards building a greater future value than our limited financial mechanisms currently allow us to conceive.

> "This is the first age that's ever paid much attention to the future, which is a little ironic since we may not have one."
> Arthur C. Clarke

Further reading (also see p.40)
1. Stern Review: The Economics of Climate Change
2. Currency Solutions for a Wiser World, Bernard Lietaer
3. World Values Survey

Discounting the discount rate 33

BIG IDEAS
FOR A SUSTAINABLE FUTURE

7/7

Calm down - it's only lustrum trading

Ever wondered why, if markets are so rational, there is so much talk of 'market confidence' and 'market sentiment'? Recent times have shown the clearest indication yet of the real power within our societies. The eurozone crisis has been precipitated by credit rating concerns and banks have failed to pass on the bounty of quantitative easing to businesses which make actual stuff. Politicians, technocrats and commentators have paid attention to only one constituency: the markets.

While this is undoubtedly bizarre, it might make sense if the markets could be said to be more rational, more objective or somehow more able to take decisions for the common good than politicians and others who might be said to have narrow or subjective agendas. Yet markets are not objective – in any way. They are not even supposed to be. Their goal is to seek profit, and often profit lies in market movement and, if you are a hedge fund, in volatility. As with any crowd behaviour, market players move relative to the herd, not through rationality. Markets are innately hysterical, not rational.

Let's take a recent example. In 2011, the UK bank Lloyds temporarily lost its CEO, who took a leave of absence due to overwork. The market reaction? Lloyds stock immediately lost 25% of its value. But what had really changed in the fundamentals of the business? Had 25% of its mortgage customers defaulted? Had bad debts increased? No, the underlying nature and purpose of the business was unchanged from the previous day. All that changed is that one man in a suit decided he needed a break. It's not really news, is it?

This is not to say that profit warnings and temporarily departing men in suits do not have some relationship to the future viability of a business; it's just that markets are unable to act proportionately because of the herd mentality. No one wants to be left behind so

34 Calm down - it's only lustrum trading

Calm down - it's only lustrum trading

It's time to move away from market hysteria, market sentiment and market confidence

everyone stampedes and people get crushed underfoot.

Sustainability requires long-term thinking
It's time to move away from market hysteria, market sentiment and market confidence. Such emotionally-volatile behaviour does not deliver the rational, logical, evidentially-based decision making that ought to be at the heart of building and maintaining the security and prosperity of the human species.

All the time short-term profit taking provides overwhelmingly larger rewards than long-term stewardship, sustainability will never be a priority for either companies or markets. Yet, abolishing quarterly reports – as suggested by John Kay's review[1] of how the equity market functions in the UK – does not go far enough, not by a long shot. Longer timescale solutions are required.

So, what to do?
One provocative proposal is to try to minimise the sub-second hysteria of the recent years in finance by radically restricting trading in shares and, through this, allowing companies to respond to the fundamentals of resource supply, customer demand and wider environmental and social trends without the distractions of the emotional meltdowns of the market.

Shares for each listed company should be traded once every five years, on one day, three months after the company makes its 'lustrum' (5 yearly) dividend.

Companies should report their ecological, social and economic performance annually, yet their decision making should not be affected by share trading which acts only in the interests of share traders, not in the interests of the company, the economy, the planet, society at large or even the real asset owners, share and pension holders.

Naysayers may argue that five years presents a cover which would allow all sorts of dodgy company behaviours and that the scrutiny of the market presents a guard against nefarious activity. However, if that were true, then our current market would bear this out – and it doesn't. Companies will continue to rise and fall, through fair means or foul under lustrum trading, but the overall outcome just might be a more sustainable one. This shouldn't put all investors out of work or prevent individuals from buying and selling shares. On any given day a multitude of companies will have shares available to trade, just not all of them all of the time.

We have to find our way away from hysteria and act to design markets and economies which automatically value and reward long-term success, stewardship and social utility. Trading a company's shares once every five years might be a valuable contribution to this goal. The idea might not be bulletproof, but it is interesting.

Further reading (also see p.40)
1. Kay review of UK equity markets and long-term decision making

Glossary

Stock and flow (reading 3)
A stock is a resource or reserve that, through its existence, can give rise to outputs or flows that do not diminish the quantity or quality of the underlying stock. A simple metaphor of this would be a bank account, whose deposit is the stock, and interest arising from that deposit is the flow.

The going concern principle (3)
A principle from accounting practice which assumes a company will continue to operate in the foreseeable future.

Market bubbles (5)
A stock market phenomenon that occurs when prices for assets rise substantially above the fundamental value of that asset. Bubbles usually presage crashes.

Fungible (5)
The capacity for something to be considered interchangeable.

Net present value (6)
An accounting term to refer to the present value of an investment's expected cash inflows minus the costs of acquiring the investment.

Discount rate (6)
A financial term that refers to the interest rate used to discount a stream of future cash flows to their present value.

Cost-benefit principle (6)
A process for calculating and comparing benefits and costs of a project, decision or policy in order to analyse its overall financial impact.

Demurrage (6)
A reverse interest rate. Demurrage is the cost associated with owning or holding currency over a given period.

The UN Sustainable Development Goals – cross reference table

The following table presents an overview of the way in which the Towards 9 Billion books cross reference with each of the UN's Sustainable Development Goals (SDGs). The SDGs have replaced the UN's Millennium Development Goals as globally-shared targets for global development to tackle issues relating to structural inequality, poverty, energy, water, climate and other key challenges for both people and planet.

As with anything in sustainability, there are few topics that are completely separate from each other. All our Towards 9 Billion ideas have the same general goal as the SDGs: to support and drive the delivery of a sustainable equitable world. However, we thought that a simple overview of which book speaks to which goal(s), and to what extent, would be helpful.

Key
- • Partial coverage or alignment
- • • Significant coverage or alignment
- • • • Complete coverage or alignment

SDG number	Book: 1	2	3	4	5
1. End poverty in all its forms everywhere	• •		•		
2. End hunger, achieve food security and improved nutrition, and promote sustainable agriculture	•		•	•	
3. Ensure healthy lives and promote wellbeing for all at all ages	• • •		•	•	
4. Ensure inclusive and equitable quality education and promote lifelong learning opportunities for all	•		•		
5. Achieve gender equality and empower all women and girls	•		•		
6. Ensure availability and sustainable management of water and sanitation for all			• •	•	
7. Ensure access to affordable, reliable, sustainable and modern energy for all	•	• • •	•	•	
8. Promote sustained, inclusive and sustainable economic growth, productive employment, and decent work for all	• • •	• •	• • •	• • •	
9. Build resilient infrastructure, promote inclusive and sustainable industrialisation, and foster innovation	•	• • •	• • •	• • •	
10. Reduce inequality within and among countries	• • •		•	•	
11. Make cities and human settlements inclusive, safe, resilient and sustainable	•	•	•		
12. Ensure sustainable consumption and production patterns	• • •	• • •	• • •	• • •	
13. Take urgent action to combat climate change and its impacts	•	• •	•	•	
14. Conserve and sustainably use the oceans, seas and marine resources for sustainable development			• •	•	
15. Protect, restore and promote sustainable use of terrestrial ecosystems, sustainably manage forests, combat desertification and halt and reverse land degradation, and halt biodiversity loss	• • •	•	• • •	•	
16. Promote peaceful and inclusive societies for sustainable development, provide access to justice for all and build effective, accountable and inclusive institutions at all levels	• •		• • •	•	•
17. Strengthen the means of implementation and revitalise the global partnership for sustainable development	• • •	• • •	• • •	• • •	• • •

Further reading

What's the point of capitalism? (reading 2)

1. Millennium-project.org. (2017). 15 Global Challenges. [online] Available at: http://www.millennium-project.org/millennium/challenges.html [Accessed 29 Aug. 2017].

2. World Economic Forum (2014). Global Risks 2014 Insight Report. The Sutton Trust submission to the Milburn Commission on access to the professions http://www3.weforum.org/docs/WEF_GlobalRisks_Report_2014.pdf [Accessed 29 Aug. 2017].

3. Piketty, T. and Goldhammer, A. (2014). Capital in the twenty-first century. Harvard University Press.

4. Hutton, W. (2017). Capitalism simply isn't working and here are the reasons why | Will Hutton. [online] the Guardian. Available at: http://www.theguardian.com/commentisfree/2014/apr/12/capitalism-isnt-working-thomas-piketty [Accessed 29 Aug. 2017].

5. Fuentes-Nieva, R. and Galasso, N. (2017). Working for the Few: Political capture and economic inequality. [online] Policy & Practice. Available at: http://policy-practice.oxfam.org.uk/publications/working-for-the-few-political-capture-and-economic-inequality-311312 [Accessed 29 Aug. 2017].

6. Sutton Trust (2009). The Educational Backgrounds of Leading Lawyers, Journalists, Vice Chancellors, Politicians, Medics and Chief Executives. The Sutton Trust submission to the Milburn Commission on access to the professions. Available at: http://www.suttontrust.com/wp-content/uploads/2009/04/ST_MilburnSubmission.pdf [Accessed 29 Aug. 2017].

Planetisation of finance: the Earth as a going concern (3)

1. Costanza, R., d'Arge, R., de Groot, R., Farber, S., Grasso, M., Hannon, B., Limburg, K., Naeem, S., O'Neill, R., Paruelo, J., Raskin, R., Sutton, P. and van den Belt, M. (2017). The value of the world's ecosystem services and natural capital.

2. TEEB. (2017). The Economics of Ecosystems and Biodiversity - TEEB. [online] Available at: http://www.teebweb.org/ [Accessed 29 Aug. 2017].

3. Naturalcapitalcoalition.org. (2017). Natural Capital Coalition. [online] Available at: http://www.naturalcapitalcoalition.org/ [Accessed 29 Aug. 2017].

4. Sustainability Accounting Standards Board (2013). Conceptual Framework of the Sustainability Accounting Standards Board. Available at: http://www.sasb.org/wp-content/uploads/2013/10/SASB-Conceptual-Framework-Final-Formatted-10-22-13.pdf [Accessed 29 Aug. 2017].

5. International Integrated Reporting Council (2013). Capitals Background Paper for <IR> Available at: http://integratedreporting.org/wp-content/uploads/2013/03/IR-Background-Paper-Capitals.pdf [Accessed 29 Aug. 2017].

6. Terrafiniti.com (2016). Terrafiniti - sustainability R&D - Earth Public Offering. [online] Terrafiniti. Available at: https://www.terrafiniti.com/towards-9-billion/earth-public-offering/ [Accessed 29 Aug. 2017].

7. Financial Reporting Council (1994). The Going Concern Basis in Financial Reports. Available at: https://www.frc.org.uk/Our-Work/Publications/APB/SAS-130-The-Going-Concern-Basis-in-Financial-State.pdf [Accessed 29 Aug. 2017].

8. Bragg, S. and Bragg, S. (2017). The going concern principle. [online] AccountingTools. Available at: http://www.accountingtools.com/going-concern-principle [Accessed 29 Aug. 2017].

9. Jane Gleeson-White (2017). Six Capitals: The revolution capitalism has to have – or can accountants save the planet?. [online] Available at: http://bookishgirl.com.au/six-capitals-the-revolution-capitalism-has-to-have-or-can-accountants-save-the-planet/ [Accessed 29 Aug. 2017].

Sensational! Against the tide of shallow value (5)

1. Stern School of Business, New York University (n/d). Market Bubbles. [online] Available at: http://pages.stern.nyu.edu/~adamodar/New_Home_Page/invfables/bubbles.htm [Accessed 29 Aug. 2017].

2. McIntosh, A. (2008). Hell and High Water: Climate Change, Hope and the Human Condition, Birlinn, Edinburgh, ISBN 978 1 84158 622 9.

3. Pierson, P. and Hacker, J. (2017). What Krugman & Stiglitz Can Tell Us. [online] The New York Review of Books. Available at: http://www.nybooks.com/articles/archives/2012/sep/27/what-krugman-stiglitz-can-tell-us/?pagination=false [Accessed 29 Aug. 2017].

4. The Price of Inequality: How Today's Divided Society Endangers Our Future, Joseph E. Stiglitz

5. John Kay. (2017). The parable of the ox - John Kay. [online] Available at: http://www.johnkay.com/2012/07/25/the-parable-of-the-ox [Accessed 29 Aug. 2017].

6. Global Justice Now. (2017). Food speculation. [online] Available at: http://www.globaljustice.org.uk/food-speculation [Accessed 29 Aug. 2017]. Food speculation, Global Justice Now

Discounting the discount rate (6)

1. Stern Review: The Economics of Climate Change (2006). Available at: http://webarchive.nationalarchives.gov.uk/+/http:/www.hm-treasury.gov.uk/media/4/3/Executive_Summary.pdf [Accessed 29 Aug. 2017].

2. Currency Solutions for a Wiser World, Bernard Lietaer (2017). Economic Crisis Currency Strategies and Solutions. [online] Available at: http://www.lietaer.com/ [Accessed 29 Aug. 2017].

3. World Values Survey (2017). WVS Database. [online] Available at: http://www.worldvaluessurvey.org/wvs.jsp [Accessed 29 Aug. 2017].

Calm down - it's only lustrum trading (6)

1. UK Government (2012). Kay review of UK equity markets and long-term decision making - GOV.UK. [online] Available at: https://www.gov.uk/government/consultations/the-kay-review-of-uk-equity-markets-and-long-term-decision-making [Accessed 29 Aug. 2017].

This page has been left blank intentionally

But you could use it to plan the next sustainable economic paradigm ...

Printed in Great Britain
by Amazon